Watch It Grow

A Sunflower's Life

Nancy Dickmann

Heinemann Library
Chicago, Illinois

www.heinemannraintree.com
Visit our website to find out
more information about
Heinemann-Raintree books.

To order:
☎ Phone 888-454-2279
💻 Visit www.heinemannraintree.com
   to browse our catalog and order online.

Edited by Rebecca Rissman, Nancy Dickmann, and Catherine Veitch
Designed by Joanna Hinton-Malivoire
Picture research by Mica Brancic
Production by Victoria Fitzgerald
Originated by Capstone Global Library Ltd
Printed and bound in the United States
of America, North Mankato, MN.

14 13 12 11 10
10 9 8 7 6 5 4 3 2 1

Library of Congress Cataloging-in-Publication Data
Dickmann, Nancy.
  A sunflower's life / Nancy Dickmann. -- 1st ed.
    p. cm. -- (Watch it grow)
  Includes bibliographical references and index.
  ISBN 978-1-4329-4144-4 (hc) -- ISBN 978-1-4329-4153-6 (pb) 1.
Sunflowers--Life cycles--Juvenile literature. I. Title. II. Series: Dickmann,
Nancy. Watch it grow.
  QK495.C74D3486 2020
  583'.99--dc22
                              2009049161

102010
005953RP

Acknowledgments
We would would like to thank the following for permission to reproduce
photographs: iStockphoto pp. **4** (© Daniel MAR), **6** (© Feng Yu), **8**
(© moshimochi), **9** (© Terje Borud), **11** (© Mary Bustraan), **13** (yellowiris),
16 (© ra-photos), **17** (© Andrey Stratilatov), **18** (© Kathy Dewar),
19 (© Ints Vikmanis), **20** (© Yuri Maryunin), **21** (© LyaC), **22 right**
(© Mary Bustraan), **22 top** (© Feng Yu), **22 left** (© ra-photos), **23 middle
top** (Arlindo 71), **23 middle bottom** (© Terje Borud); Photolibrary p. **12**
(Garden Picture Library/© Kate Gadsby); Shutterstock pp. **5** (© irin-K),
7 (CamPot), **10** (© Evon Lim Seo Ling), **14** (© Tropinina Olga), **15**
(© kukuruxa), **22 bottom** (© Tropinina Olga), **23 bottom** (© Evon Lim
Seo Ling), **23 top** (© Tropinina Olga).

Front cover photograph (main) of a field of sunflowers reproduced with
permission of iStockphoto (ooyoo). Front cover photograph (inset) of a
close-up of sunflower seeds reproduced with permission of Shutterstock
(© BW Folsom). Back cover photograph of a sunflower shoot reproduced
with permission of iStockphoto (© Mary Bustraan).

The publisher would like to thank Nancy Harris for her assistance in the
preparation of this book.

Every effort has been made to contact copyright holders of material
reproduced in this book. Any omissions will be rectified in subsequent
printings if notice is given to the publisher.

Contents

Life Cycles

All living things have a life cycle.

A sunflower has a life cycle.

seed

A sunflower starts as a tiny seed.

The seed grows into a sunflower.

The sunflower grows new seeds.

The life cycle starts again.

Seeds and Shoots

A sunflower seed grows in the ground.

root

Roots grow down from the seed into the ground.

shoot

A shoot grows from the seed.

leaves

Leaves grow from the shoot.

Becoming a Flower

The sunflower plant needs water and sunlight to grow.

The sunflower plant grows taller.

bud

A bud grows at the top of the plant.

petals

The bud opens. There are yellow petals inside.

Making Seeds

The flower turns towards the Sun.

A bee comes to feed on the flower.
The bee has pollen on it.

new seeds

The pollen helps make new sunflower seeds grow in the flower.

The flower dies.

Some seeds fall to the ground.

The life cycle starts again.

Life Cycle of a Sunflower

1 A sunflower seed grows in the ground.

2 A shoot and leaves grow from the seed.

3 A bud grows at the top of the plant.

4 The bud opens into a sunflower.

22

Picture Glossary

bud part of a plant that opens into a flower

pollen yellow powder inside a flower

root part of a plant that grows underground. Roots take up water for the plant to use.

shoot small green stem that grows from a seed

Index

Notes to Parents and Teachers

Before reading

Ask the children if they have ever grown flowers. Ask them if they know what a plant needs to grow. Show them some sunflower seeds. What else do they know that grows from seeds?

After reading

• Put the children into groups and give them three yogurt cups (to use as pots), some soil, and three sunflower seeds. Show them how to plant the seeds and label the pots 1, 2, and 3. Tell them to put pot 1 in sunlight and water it every day, to put pot 2 in sunlight but give it no water, and to put pot 3 in a dark place away from sunlight and water it every day. Ask them to keep a record of what happens to their seeds. Ask them which seed did best. Why do they think this happened and what can they conclude about plants' needs?

• Tell the children that seeds are a good energy food. Roast some sunflower seeds and eat them together as a healthy snack.